THE LOVE ONE

DEVELOPING UNITY
UPHOLDING THE ONENESS GOD GIVES ME WITH OTHERS

A Bible Study by

Churches Alive!

MINISTERING TO THE CHURCHES OF THE WORLD
600 Meridian Avenue, Suite 200
San Jose, California 95126-3427

Published by

BRINGING TRUTH TO LIFE
NavPress Publishing Group
P.O. Box 35001, Colorado Springs, Colorado 80935

*Because we share kindred aims for helping local churches fulfill Christ's Great
Commission to "go and make disciples," NavPress and Churches Alive have
joined efforts on certain strategic publishing projects that are intended to bring
effective disciplemaking resources into the service of the local church.*

*For more than a decade, Churches Alive has teamed up with churches of all
denominations to establish vigorous disciplemaking ministries. At the same time,
NavPress has focused on publishing Bible studies, books, and other resources
that have grown out of The Navigators' 50 years of disciplemaking experience.*

*Now, together, we're working to offer special products like this one that are
designed to stimulate a deeper, more fruitful commitment to Christ in the local
gatherings of His Church.*

The LOVE ONE ANOTHER *series was written by Russ Korth, Ron Wormser, Jr., and
Ron Wormser, Sr. of Churches Alive. Many individuals from both Churches
Alive and NavPress contributed greatly in bringing this project to publication.*

Contents

It may seem like poor mathematics; but when one is added to one in marriage, they equal one. This is the highest level of unity in interpersonal relationships and a living illustration of the spiritual oneness we have with Christ.

LESSON ONE

Two Become One

▼

1 If married, relate the most meaningful part of your wedding ceremony. If single, relate the most meaningful part of a wedding ceremony you observed.

2 What purposes for marriage are suggested in Genesis 1:26-28 and Genesis 2:18-25? (KJV—"meet" = "fit")

3 Use the concepts from the passages below and write out what you think "two shall become one" means. (Matthew 19:5-6, Ephesians 5:31-32)

4 What view of sex is presented in Hebrews 13:4?

5 Why is adultery a violation of the "two shall become one" concept? (1 Corinthians 6:15-20)

6 What are some practical reasons for not committing adultery? (Proverbs 6:23-35)

7 What do you feel are some other implications of the fact that two become one in marriage?

8 What did Jesus teach about divorce? (Matthew 5:31-32, 19:3-9)

9 What did Paul teach about divorce? (1 Corinthians 7:10-15)

10 If married, choose a passage from Song of Songs (also called Song of Solomon) that expresses how you feel about your spouse. If single, choose a passage from Song of Songs and tell how it reveals the unity of marriage.

Functioning as One

▼

1 Name an activity that requires exactly two people to perform and use it to illustrate functioning as one in marriage.

2 What are some of the implications of the rhetorical question in Amos 3:3?

3 In what ways are men and women different, and in what ways are they the same? (1 Corinthians 11:8-12)

DIFFERENT	SAME

4 Read Ephesians 5:21-33.

   a. What is the responsibility of the husband?

   b. What is the responsibility of the wife?

   c. What do you think you should do if your mate is not fulfilling his or her responsibility? Why?

5 a. What responsibilities for marriage are given in 1 Peter 3:1-7? (Husbands—verse 7; wives—verses 1-4)

   b. First Peter 3:1-7 begins with the phrase "in the same way" or "likewise." To what concept do these phrases refer? (1 Peter 2:19-25)

c. What does this indicate about the degree of commitment you should have to your marriage responsibilities?

6 Choose three characteristics of a virtuous woman from Proverbs 31:10-31 and list them in the chart. Next to each, list one thing you think a husband could do that would help his wife be that kind of woman.

CHARACTERISTICS OF A VIRTUOUS WOMAN	HUSBAND'S CONTRIBUTION

7 Read about Aquila and Priscilla in Acts 18, Romans 16:3, and 1 Corinthians 16:19. In what ways did they function as one? List both the ways stated and also what you infer from the passages.

8 How does the scriptural view of marriage compare with the philosophy, "I'll do my part if you'll do yours"?

Family Foundations

1 What is one way you benefited from your family relationships as you grew up?

2 What do the following passages indicate about the importance of the family unit?

Genesis 12:3

Exodus 12:3

1 Samuel 20:28-29

John 19:25-27

3 What is God's order for the family? (1 Corinthians 11:3)

4 Read Colossians 3:18-21.

   a. To whom is the command given?

   b. What is the command?

   c. Why should the command be obeyed?

5 a. Read Psalm 127 and list at least four things it teaches
      about the family.

b. In what ways do you see children as being like arrows, as mentioned in Psalm 127:4?

6 Read 1 Timothy 3:4-5. What do you conclude about the emphasis you should place on your family?

7 Read Genesis 37.

a. What do you think were major factors producing the animosity Joseph's brothers had toward him?

b. What instructions would you have given to these people?

■ Joseph

■ His brothers

■ His parents

8 What do you think God would say to a person who has a strained relationship with any member of his or her immediate family?

Family trees, family skeletons, family feuds, family circle, family resemblance, family night—all speak of the obvious unity of the family. To realize the full value of this family unit, every member must fulfill his or her role and responsibilities as ordained by God.

LESSON FOUR
Family Responsibilities

1 a. When you were growing up, what was a responsibility you had and hated to do?

b. How is that job handled in your household now?

2 What responsibilities for parents are indicated in each of the following passages?

2 Corinthians 12:14-15

Ephesians 6:4

1 Thessalonians 2:7-8,11

3 What are major topics on which parental teaching should center?

Deuteronomy 6:4-7

Proverbs 1:7-8

Proverbs 3:5-6

Proverbs 5:1-2

4 According to each of the following verses, why is discipline important?

Proverbs 19:18

Proverbs 29:17

Ecclesiastes 8:11

5 a. If you could guarantee your children were going to gain three things from you, what would they be?

b. What are you doing on a consistent basis in your family to help your children develop in one of these areas?

c. How do you need to reorganize your schedule to allow for the development of this area?

6 What responses should children have toward their parents?

Proverbs 13:1

Proverbs 15:5

Proverbs 19:26

Proverbs 20:20

Ephesians 6:1-3

7 Read Jeremiah 35.

a. What did God tell Jeremiah to do? (Verse 2)

b. How did the Rechabites respond to Jeremiah's offer as he obeyed God? Why? (Verse 6)

c. Was there anything intrinsically wrong with the actions the Rechabites were told not to do? (Verses 6-7)

d. What significance did God put on their response? (Verses 14,16)

e. What did God promise to them as a result? (Verses 18-19)

f. How can the principle illustrated in this event be applied to your life?

8 Why do you think family attitudes should characterize your relationship to other people in your church? (1 Timothy 5:1-2)

Unity is not established by people looking or acting alike.
The unity of a local church is in the mutual love, care, and
concern for one another. Dynamic fellowship and close
interpersonal relationships are keys to this unity in practice.

Dynamic Fellowship

▼

1 What fellowship activities in your church do you enjoy the most? Tell why.

2 Using your own words, rewrite Psalm 133:1.

3 What must be true of your life before you can have fellowship with other believers? (1 John 1:3-7)

4 Rate each of the five things below according to their importance to having good fellowship. Number 1 is most important, and number 5 is least important.

- Doctrinal agreement
- Doing the right activities together
- Individually being in fellowship with God
- Having affection for one another
- Honestly admitting shortcomings

5 a. List the actions that characterized the fellowship of the early church from Acts 2:42-47 in the chart below. In the second column list activities from your church that parallel those found in Acts 2.

ACTS 2 ACTIVITIES	ACTIVITIES IN YOUR CHURCH

b. From this exercise, what do you find to be the most encouraging thing about your church?

c. What is the best suggestion you have for your church?

6 What mutual activities that characterize dynamic fellowship are mentioned in the following verses?

Romans 12:10

Romans 13:8

Romans 14:13

Romans 14:19

Romans 15:7

Romans 16:16

7 Choose one activity from the list above and give one suggestion you think would improve the quality of this activity in
your church.

8 a. What two activities are indicated for the local church in
Hebrews 10:25?

b. How are you involved in your church in fulfilling these
activities?

c. What should result from these activities? (Hebrews 10:24)

d. What evidence do you have that you are producing these results?

9 According to 1 Corinthians 6:1-8, what actions should be taken to resolve disagreements between believers within your church?

10 What effect do you think dynamic fellowship has on those who observe it?

Lesson Six
Deepening Relationships

▼

1 Name three people outside your immediate family with whom you have had a very close relationship. For each one list one experience you had together that deepened your relationship.

2 What is true of relationships between growing Christians? (Ephesians 4:15-16)

3 Think about this statement: *I find it hard to be honest with others in my church fellowship because. . . .* (Check all of the answers that apply.)

☐ They won't understand.
☐ They will be horrified after finding out about me.
☐ They don't trust others.
☐ They won't like what I say.
☐ I can't say it in love.
☐ If I do, they will preach at me.
☐ Other (write your own):

4 What does James 5:16 command?

5 a. What needs did Paul indicate he had in 2 Timothy 4:9-13?

,

b. How do you think sharing these needs affected his relationship with Timothy?

6 What principles of developing relationships do you see in the following references?

1 Corinthians 9:20-23

Hebrews 13:3

7 Read 1 Samuel 18:1-4, 19:1-7. What are some of the things Jonathan did which demonstrated his close relationship with David?

8 a. What are some ways you can develop close relationships with others in your church?

b. How are your relationships to people in your church like your family relationships?

You can't see the unity of Christians by looking at the outside of them. They have different jobs, talents and personalities. But all are united in Christ—inside each one is the presence of Almighty God.

LESSON SEVEN
Unity of Believers

▼

1 If you were to go to another culture to minister to believers, where would you choose to go? Why?

2 Ephesians 4:4-6 lists seven "ones." What are they, and how do you feel each contributes to the oneness believers have in Christ?

"ONES"	CONTRIBUTION TO UNITY

3 What instruction is associated with this list? (Ephesians 4:3)

4 Read Ephesians 2:11-19.

    a. What was the distinction between Jews and Gentiles (nonJews) before Christ?

    b. What is the relationship between Jewish and Gentile believers now?

5 Read John 17:20-23.

    a. What did Jesus request in prayer?

    b. What is the basis for the fulfillment of His request?

c. What would be the results of the fulfillment?

d. What is God doing toward fulfilling that request?
   (Colossians 3:10-11)

6 What can you do as an individual or as a group that would contribute toward the fulfillment of Jesus' request?

7 Read 1 Corinthians 1:9-13, 3:1-7 and list the following.

ATTITUDES AND ACTIONS ASSOCIATED WITH UNITY	ATTITUDES AND ACTIONS ASSOCIATED WITH DISUNITY

8 Next to the six topics below list the attitudes and actions from Colossians 3:12-16 you feel correspond to each. (KJV—"bowels" = "heart")

Forgiving

Understanding

Honoring

Submitting

Communicating

Contributing

9 What is one way God expects you to express your unity with believers of other denominations, other races, or other cultures?

God did not design a machine to produce people who
are all alike. All have individual differences,
but all are created in God's own image.

LESSON EIGHT
Universal Human Dignity

▼

1 What are some of the things that make people distinct from the rest of creation? (Genesis 1:26-28, 2:15-25)

2 How do the distinctives listed above show that God has given each person dignity?

3 What are some of the similarities you can think of between God and people that indicate you are created in God's image?

4 Since people are created in God's image, how should you treat others?

Genesis 9:6

James 3:8-10

5 From your study thus far, explain why you should not be prejudiced against any person.

6 In Acts 17:24-31, what things did Paul state are the same for everyone?

7 What are some characteristics shared by everyone?

Proverbs 16:9

Proverbs 21:2

Proverbs 27:19

Ephesians 5:29

James 4:14

8 On the basis of the above list, how do you think you should react to others?

9 What is one way to respect the dignity of those who live ungodly and immoral lives?

Universal Human Need

▼

1 Rewrite Romans 3:9,19 in your own words.

2 What steps leading to spiritual death are given in James 1:13-15?

3 From Ecclesiastes 1:16–2:11 list three ways Solomon sought fulfillment in life apart from God. Then describe a modern-day counterpart for each activity on your list.

ATTEMPTS FOR FULFILLMENT	COUNTERPART TODAY

4 a. After all these experiences, what was Solomon's final conclusion? (Ecclesiastes 12:13)

   b. What reasons could you give for reaching the same conclusion?

5 Read John 8:1-11.

   a. What if you could have been a person in the crowd? Describe the changing emotions you think someone might have felt as this event took place.

   b. What application can you make as a result of studying this passage?

6 From John 17:15-16 and 1 Corinthians 5:9-10, how do you feel you should relate to nonChristians?

7 a. Read Matthew 5:38-48. Choose one of the commands about relating to nonbelievers and describe how it could be applied in an existing situation in your life.

b. Why is it reasonable for you to love others in this way? (1 John 4:16-19)

8 What are two warnings Paul gave about relationships with nonChristians?

1 Corinthians 15:33

2 Corinthians 6:14

9 Describe the elements of successful witnessing from Colossians 4:2-6.

10 What are some present-day examples of people speaking both with grace and having their speech "seasoned with salt"? (Colossians 4:6)

11 a. Describe your current relationship to some nonChristians.

b. How are you involved in the Great Commission? (Matthew 28:18-20)